EXPLORING BURRATOR
A Dartmoor Reservoir

By Paul Rendell

First published in 2007 by the Dartmoor Company.
The Coach House, Tramlines, Okehampton, Devonshire. EX20 1EH
Telephone: 01837 54727

Copyright   © Paul Rendell 2007

ISBN 978-0-9555 150-0-2

All rights reserved. No part of this book may be reproduced or transmitted in any form or by any means, electronic or mechanical, including photocopying, recording or by any information storage or retrieval system, without permission from the publisher.

Printed by:
GTI, Okehampton, EX20 1DJ

CONTENTS

Acknowledgements 4

Introduction 5

The building of Burrator Reservoir 7

The Farms 10

Other buildings 35

Other items of interest 40

Exploring the area 43

Appendix – Tenants of Farms 54

Bibliography 61

Index 63

The Author 64

ACKNOWLEDGEMENTS

Edward Bayly, Kate Brewer, Simon Butler, Simon Dell, Elizabeth Edmondson, Moya Eley, Dave German, Pauline Greenwood, Mike Lang, William Legassick, Pauline Hamilton-Leggett, Peter Hamilton-Leggett, Trevor James, Phil Newman, Nelson Palmer, Millie Matthews (nee Pearse), John Pearse, Mary Palmer, Hilda Piper (nee Watkins), Gerald Taylor, John Weir.

Photographs are acknowledged individually in most instances but thanks go to Hilda Piper, Hugh Robinson, Dave German, Paul London, Alan Lomax, Des Puttick, June Puttick and Simon Butler of the Dartmoor Trust for help in locating some of the photographs.

SPECIAL THANKS TO:
My dad, Derek, who took me to Burrator at a very young age and gave me my love for Dartmoor and taught me how to take photographs. Sadly he did not live long enough to see this book published.

DEDICATION
This book is dedicated to my special companion and friend Pauline, who has helped me with this book and tramped many miles across Dartmoor with me.

FRONT COVER - Burrator Resevoir by Paul Rendell.

BACK COVER - Middleworth Barn, Deancombe Valley by Pauline Greenwood.

INTRODUCTION

Burrator Reservoir attracts thousands of visitors every year. It was built just over 100 years ago as a water supply for Plymouth. Yet the history of the area goes back to the Bronze Age, when 'round houses' were built as dwellings. Later on 'longhouses' were built, where animals and humans lived under the same roof. As the farms became larger small communities grew up around them. In the 19th century these rural communities provided the farmers with most of their daily needs; the nearest villages were Sheepstor, Meavy and Walkhampton. Tavistock, was the nearest market town, Plymouth was very rarely visited.

There are a number of rivers and streams flowing into Burrator Reservoir, including the River Meavy, Hart Tor Brook, Newleycombe Lake, Narrator Brook, Combeshead Brook and Deancombe Brook. Many of the farms were within these river valleys and used the higher ground for the grazing of animals. Also within these valleys, tin was worked from at least the 15th century and there were many buildings associated with these activities, from dwellings to mills. The area covered in this book is within the three parishes of Sheepstor, Walkhampton and a part of Meavy.

The aim of this booklet is to help you explore the area around Burrator Reservoir including the valleys of the Meavy, Newleycombe, and Narrator. The information within this book has been gathered from many sources both documentary and oral, and is the result of about twenty years research. It all began with trips to the area with my parents. I grew to love the place and began asking questions and started researching for this book. Over the years different place names have occurred and here I have used the name as written in the document. In these pages I have tried to explain some of the things to be found and the brief history of most of the farms within the area. It would take a book many times larger than this one to relate everything to be seen and the full history of the 22 dwellings. I have concluded with a description of two suggested circular walks, passing many of the places mentioned in this book. I hope that I have achieved my aim in helping you to explore the history around Burrator.

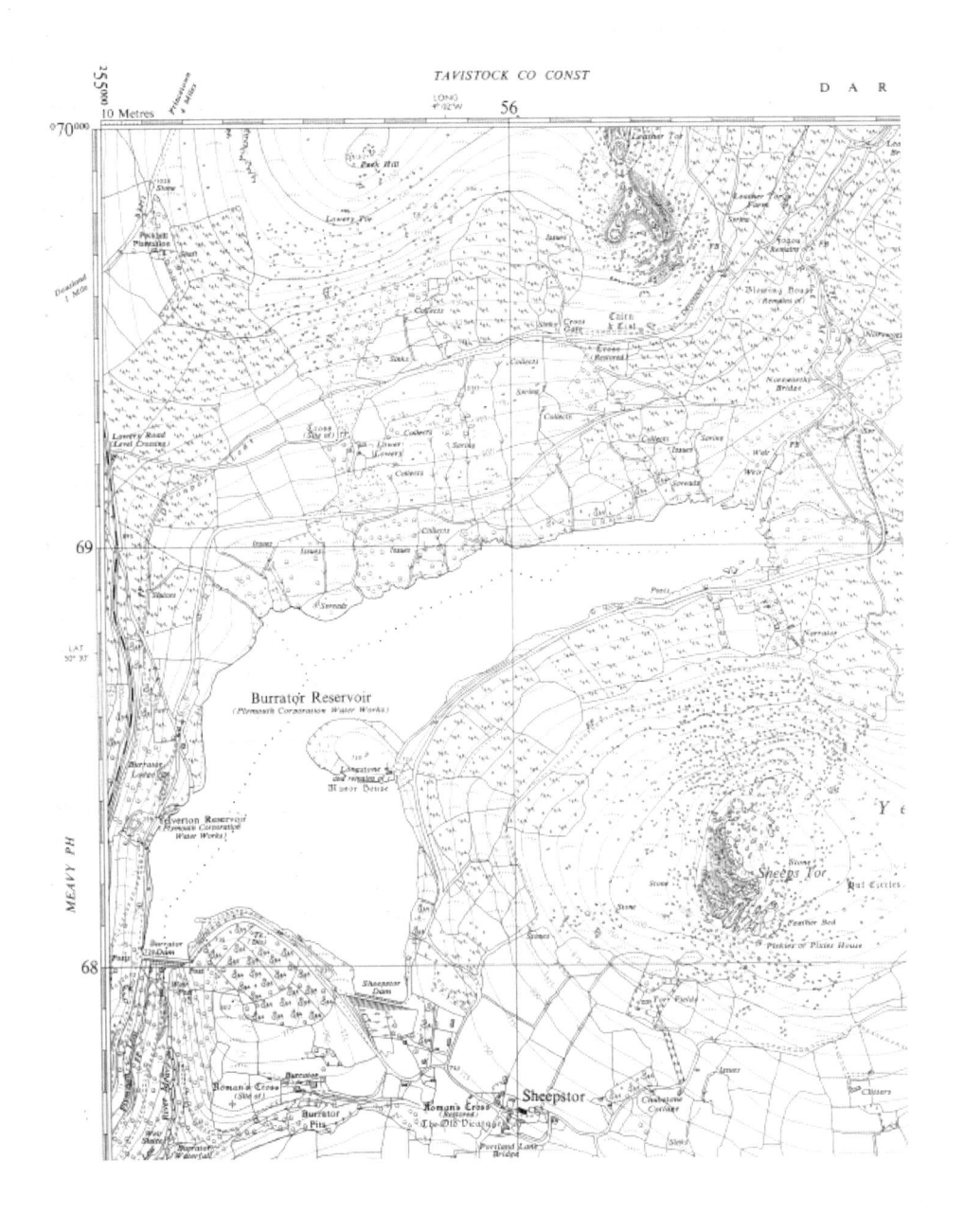

"Reproduced from 1954 Ordnance Survey map with kind permission of the Ordnance Survey"

THE BUILDING OF BURRATOR RESERVOIR

The reservoir was built during the 1880's as a water supply for Plymouth but the story goes back much further to the 1500's when Sir Francis Drake was involved in bringing water to the town. In 1559 Plymouth Corporation decided to extract fresh water from Dartmoor and awarded the contract to a Mr Forsland who ran a company in Bovey Tracey which specialised in the construction of aqueducts and leats for tin miners. Little progress was made until 1585 when Elizabeth 1st passed a Parliamentary Act which allowed the Corporation to take water via a leat from the River Meavy. It was not until December 1590 that work started on this leat. Francis Drake was by this time the Mayor of Plymouth, a Member of Parliament, and a civil engineer who owned many mills in and round Plymouth, including one at Meavy. He was awarded the contract to dig the Plymouth Leat and was given £500 to pay to landowners as compensation (£100), the workforce of 30 men (£200) and the remaining £200 was to be his profit. The work was finished by 23rd April 1591, after about 19 weeks and covering a distance of 18 miles – over a mile per week! This was partly because he re-used the old Maristow Leat which saved a lot of time. This leat started near Burrator and ran to Jump, now known as Roborough and was used for a mill at Maristow in the Tavy Valley.

In the 1880's it was decided to build a reservoir to replace the Plymouth Leat, also known as Drake's Leat. The leat was freezing over in the winter and with the population of Plymouth growing it was drying up in the summer. Burrator Gorge was the chosen site, the third place that was looked at on the River Meavy. Work started on 9th August 1893 and Edward Sanderman, aged 29 was the engineer.

*View from inside reservoir showing the
River Meavy and the temporary railway.
(Plymouth and West Devon Record Office)*

It was estimated that it would take 7 years to build but only took 5 years. Around 300 men were employed constructing the reservoir, with nearly half of them coming from the local villages of Walkhampton, Sheepstor and Meavy. Other men came from Plymouth while some were from Wales and Ireland. Two dams were built, Burrator, taking its name from the granite outcrop of rock nearby and the smaller earth filled embankment called Sheepstor Dam. The reservoir was opened on 21st September 1898 at a cost of £178,000, equal to around £7 million today.

In 1914 the 'Three Towns' of Plymouth, Stonehouse and Devonport were merged and once again the demand for water was greatly increased so it was decided to raise each of the dams by 10 feet at an estimated cost of £135,000. Work began in December 1923 and took 4 ½ years to complete. A temporary suspension bridge was built to allow traffic into the village of Sheepstor.

Temporary suspension bridge at Burrator Dam 1925
(Taken by Sydney Taylor © Dartmoor National Park Authority
/ Devon County Council)

Putting the finishing touches to Burrator Dam
(Plymouth and West Devon Record Office)

THE FARMS

There have always been a large number of farms within the area around Burrator. Some of them date from the 1300's and were still in use in the last century, while others just lasted around a hundred years. The history of some of the farms is well documented like Kingsett in the Newleycombe valley, but for many others there is little visible evidence on the ground of a farm ever having been there, or any documented evidence. Chipstone (approx. SX558 680) for example was thought to have stood near Redstone but Hayes wrote in 1966 'A dwelling named Chipstone to the right of the lane from Redstone to the site of Park Cottage. There is no trace of this site now, only a sand quarry in the area, and no indication on the 1887 OS 6" map'. The author has managed to find the foundation of a building, which could be Chipstone near Redstone, but it is possible it was just an outbuilding of Redstone.

Not all the farms are included in this book, a few smaller ones like Colliers (SX 582 701) are not included. Colliers is a ruined building that can be seen between Crazywell and Newleycombe farms. It was abandoned by 1840.

Maristow Estate owned most of the land during the 1800's and the farmers were tenants until the building of the reservoir when Plymouth Corporation bought the land and all the dwellings within the catchment area. When the reservoir was completed there was concern about the quality of the water and the farmers were getting the blame. Just months after the reservoir was starting to fill up there was an article in the Western Morning News on 23 November 1898 about this very matter. An un-named person from Plymouth who had seen the reservoir being built was asking why the water was very dark in colour and why it had a putrid smell. Was it because the impure earth and vegetable matter, i.e. grass, bushes etc. were left in place when they flooded the valley, or was it the drainage from about a dozen farm buildings finding its way into the water? If so at it's best, the water would be none too pure. He also wanted to know why they were letting the water out of the reservoir again.

The local paper was so concerned about this and their headline read "Burrator Reservoir – is it polluted?" They asked the Water Engineer, Mr Edward Sanderman a lot of questions and invited him to explain what was going on. He replied: *"As the reservoir started to fill up, all the grass, bushes, brambles and other vegetation growing over the land decomposed and gases were released that affected the water to a 'certain extent'. It was only vegetation, not animal matter, which could cause the problems. It had been a dry summer but there had been a number of storms with heavy rain bringing more vegetable matter into the rivers. There was nothing to worry about and there was no serious pollution."* When the reservoir was one-sixth full, because of the discoloration of the water, he let the water out again. With more heavy rain, the reservoir soon filled, and again he let the water out. The third time, when the reservoir was partially filled, the water was much clearer but Mr Sanderman decided to let the water out once more. He told the newspaper that it was now filling again, the water was very clear and he believed it would not be necessary to empty it again. He said there was very little smell.

When Mr Sanderman was asked about the pollution from the farmhouses getting into the water supplies, he answered: "The danger of water being polluted by the few homesteads which dot a portion of the watershed, if it exists at all, is no greater now than it has ever been. These farms have existed for centuries, and if there was any danger of their polluting the water there would have been some evidence of it in the past years. That this danger is more imaginary than real is proved by the analyses periodically made of the water at Head Weir, which all without exception show it to be one of the purest in the Kingdom". He pointed out some of the buildings had been abandoned and some demolished so there was less of a problem now than before. This explanation was accepted for a while but soon the people living in Plymouth complained again about the water and the poor farmers got the blame. In the end Plymouth Corporation made the farmers leave their farms. Today the land is owned by South West Water and most of the buildings are in ruins.

Combeshead (SX586 685)

This farm was mentioned in 1768 when the Walkhampton Manor Court Rolls stated "that John Giles of Combshed (sic) had died and the new tenant will be William Creber". In 1840 the farm building was in a dilapidated state and the Maristow Estate bought the property for £16.1s.11d. by which time the spelling had changed to Coomeshead. George Pengelly took over the tenancy in about 1880.

Combeshead Farm 1934
(Taken by Sydney Taylor © Dartmoor National Park Authority/ Devon County Council)

William Pengelly was running the farm in 1906 and he was there until his death. Bill, as he was known, was a 'proper' Dartmoor character and many stories are told about him. It is said he would walk the few miles to the Park Cottage Inn twice a week after work and drink a couple of pints of cider then walk home again. Once a week he would, we are told, pick up a barrel of cider and walk home with it on his back. He must have been very strong to do this but more than likely he put it on his cart and then rode home with it. One day the locals decided to play a trick on him: they switched his barrel of cider for one of water. After taking it home and before going to bed he decided to have a sip and discovered it was not even good tasting water. This Dartmoor character must have got his own back on the locals but this is not recorded.

In the 1920's William had just rendered and painted the walls of his house with black pitch when along came Plymouth Corporation, who now owned the property, and told him to leave within a year. They said that pollution from the animals and from humans was going into Burrator Reservoir and causing problems for the consumers in Plymouth. He told them that his father had farmed the land all this life and he had done the same and was not going to leave his farm. The officials tried hard to get him to leave but he declared: *"the only way you are going to get me to leave is in my coffin"*. After a lengthy debate, he was allowed to stay on the farm, but he had to get rid of his farm animals. He was allowed to grow crops to eat but the soil was not good enough for this. Potatoes were grown in one of the fields many years ago but that is all. He stayed there rent-free until he died in December 1931 at the age of 90. He was carried in his coffin to be buried at Sheepstor Churchyard.

This was the last dwelling to be occupied within the Burrator catchment area. Today there are a few ruined buildings including the farmhouse, outside toilet and a potato cave as well as track ways and a small clapper bridge over Combeshead Brook. In 1985 Goldcrest filmed 'Revolution' in a field at Combeshead Farm. There were tents and hundreds of soldiers seen in a battle. The author was a British soldier in this film.

Funeral of William (Bill) Pengelley in 1931
(Western Morning News –Paul Rendell Collection)

Classywell (SX581 701)

This farm is just below Classywell (Crazywell) Pool. The word Crazywell seems to be a 20th century name with earlier names of Classywell and Claceywell. There has been a farm here since 1565. The Walkhampton Manor Court Rolls of 1781 state that a new tenant; William Giles took over the tenancy. Just ten years later Joseph Spurr was there and paying rent of 2d per year and 5s tax. This farm was very small indeed but he was also paying rent for other farms and land within the area including East Middleworthy in the Deancombe Valley. Sometime between 1866 and 1873 the farm was abandoned and today very little remains, only part of the farmhouse and driveways can be seen.

Deancombe (SX580 688)

This is a very old farmstead. In 1317 the moormen called the valley 'Denecomb' but there was no mention of a farm. The first mention of it seems to be in the Sites & Monuments Register, when in 1450 John Shullabere of Dencomb coined 248lbs of tin at Plympton. Now part of Plymouth, Plympton was once a Stannary town. In 1582 there were two farmsteads here. John Windiatt was at East Deancombe while Robert Cockle was at West Deancombe. Roger Atwill of Willtown (now Welltown) in the parish of Walkhampton bequeathed unto Elias Giles senior the Deancombe Estate in 1797. In 1801 John King of West Deancombe was paying an annual rent of 7s. 2d. and the tax was £1.4s 0d. At around this time Maristow bought up the farms. There were still two farms being worked here until at least 1850. Maristow rebuilt East Deancombe in 1858. There used to be a date plaque here but now this is nowhere to be seen. The last tenant was George Hamlyn and he worked there until around 1910.

Deancombe Farm from Cuckoo Rock
(Paul Rendell collection)

Today there is a lot to see here including a raised vegetable garden, five surviving rick staddles which were used to store hay on and many ruined buildings including the farmhouse. There is an adit nearby which was once used to drain the small tin mine.

Deancombe Farm
(Taken by Sydney Taylor © Dartmoor National Park Authority/ Devon County Council)

Essworthy (Approx. SX555 6830)

The only farm that lies under Burrator Reservoir is Essworthy. The name Essworthy is believed to be a corruption of 'Hext's worthy'. In a Churchwarden's Account book for Sheepstor parish, there is an entry for Yeoford Farm in 1718 for paying rates, the occupier being Sarah Creber. It is not until 1728 we are able to discover the location of this property. It lists 'Yeoford alias Essery' and again in 1741 as 'Yeoford otherwise Essery'. Succeeding entries lists Yeoford until 1759. In 1746 the tenants were John Bounsall and Phillip William. Essworthy and Longstone estates merged in 1893 and George Creber was the farmer. South West Water

Records show that Plymouth Corporation owned the farm at Essworthy, the year that the reservoir was completed. The farm was then flooded never to been seen again.

Essworthy *Farm*
(Plymouth and West Devon Record Office)

Kingsett (SX576 699)

In 1333 it was listed as Kingsette and paying taxes. The Walkhampton Manor Court Rolls of April 1666 mentions Philip Cockle being at Kingsett.

In 1738 John Giles had to pay his dues to the Moorman of West Quarter for cutting tuft [peat] in the forest. It is not until the early 1800's do we get records of Kingsett. In 1801 the place was known as 'Two Kingsetts', comprising East and West Kingsett. J.M Knighton Esq. paid £2.15s.4d. for two years rent and tax. Following the death of Grace Hancock on the 20th October 1848, Kingsett became part of Sir Ralph Lopes' Maristow Estate. The property was in a terrible state of repair. It is interesting to see what work had to be done to bring the building back to a liveable condition. It cost £4. 4s. 10½ d. for mayons [mason] work, £4. 18s. 16d. for carpenters work, '£4. 12s. 6d. for the glayier [glass] work' and they must have had a new thatch put on as this cost £13. 9s. 6d. There were also gates and hedges to mend bringing the total costs to £43. 6s. 5½d. This work was done between January and May the following year for Richard Worth who took over the tenancy on 4th May 1849.

The former Mine Captain at Eylesbarrow Mine, James Deacon lived there in 1839 and for a few years afterwards. The seating plan for Walkhampton Church on 14th April 1860 shows there were two seats for Kingsett and these were reserved seats in the tenth row in the central aisle. They shared the pew with Classywell, and Newlicombe, both of which also had two seats.

John Pearse was living at the farm in 1881; he farmed 100 acres with his wife Elizabeth. The Census Returns also lists a son of five months and two servants, May (surname unreadable), age 13 and William Gill aged 15. It was John Pearse who planted that lovely beech tree in the court yard which still stands today.

Maristow Estate rentals show that in 1896 John Pearse had taken over the nearby Nosworthy Farm and was working both farms as one unit. He paid £78 rent for Kingsett and £42 for Nosworthy. In fact he was also working the land that once belonged to Classywell and Newlicombe farms. He was still there in 1912 when the Duchy asked him for help concerning a boundary dispute with Walkhampton Parish. He told them he took over Walkhampton Commons in 1866 and did not know the boundary. His brother Thomas who was born in 1887 also worked the farm and they kept around 60 Dartmoor White-faced sheep, mainly for their wool.

In the late 19th century and early 20th century Kingsett must have been a very big farm for John Pearse had around 100 head of Scottish black-faced sheep as well as rents from part of the common and took in cattle to graze. John and Thomas moved out in the early 1910s to Hernspitt in the same parish of Walkhampton.

One of the other brothers, Sam, then took over Kingsett and farmed the land despite Plymouth Corporation trying to kick him out. John Pearse died on 29th September 1917 aged 77 and is buried in Sheepstor Churchyard because although the farm was in Walkhampton parish the people associated themselves more with Sheepstor. One of his sons, also called Sam, then took over the farm until the tenancy ended in 1924.

Mrs Millie Matthews (nee Pearse) who lived at Kingsett Farm between 1905 –1924 used to ride a pony with her sister to Narrator Farm to pick up Hilda Watkins and they would all go off to Sheepstor School together. They would then leave the pony tied in a field while they were at school; at the end of the day they would ride home together. There used to be hundreds of glow-worms on the land from the farm towards Nosworthy Bridge.

Kingsett Farm 1960's
(Hugh Robinson)

The last years were a very bad time for the Pearse family. After Plymouth City Corporation bought the farm from Maristow Estate some years earlier the Pearses were not allowed to keep any animals and the Corporation finally gave them notice to quit their farm early in 1924. They were given no compensation, nor offered any accomodation or sympathy at all. The Corporate Land Agent would visit them and he would give them a dressing down because they had not yet moved. They finally moved out in September 1924 and now the farm is a ruin.

Leathertor (SX567 698)

A settlement of medieval origin first mentioned in 1362 in the Bailiff's Accounts for the Manor of Dartmoor. John Northway was charged for an acre of land at 'Leddertorre' and Robert Taverner for two acres at 'Laddertorre Comb'. This could have been just land with a dwelling. In 1511 there is mention of a farm. William & Jane Dunster leased the farm and a Knocking Mill. John Browne of Ledertorre coined tin at the Tavistock Stannary in 1523, so farmers of Leathertor must have been involved in tin mining; perhaps farming alone did not bring in enough income.

In 1785 John Atwill took over as tenant of East Leathertor and once again, as with in a lot of farmsteads, there was more than one farm there. Abraham & Robert Giles were at East Leathertor Farm between 1801-1810 while at the same period Richard Andrew was to be found paying rent for East Lowery as well as West Leathertor. Thomas Pearse took over in 1883 when the yearly rent was £131 and he stayed until 1890. The last tenant was John Lillicrap who was there until 1924 when the family moved to Walkhampton to live.

Often after buildings were abandoned the stone was sometimes recycled and this was the case at Lowery and at Leathertor. Around 1925 stone was removed from the farmhouse and used to build a summerhouse just over the hill at a dwelling called the Fold. This summerhouse was built for the children to play in. It even had a thatched roof. Today this folly is just a shell and stands on private land. It can be seen from the Princetown to Yelverton Road.

Lowery

There are many buildings known as Lowery and records show buildings called Lower Lowery, (SX 556 692), Lower Lowery Houses, Middle Lowery, Higher Lowery (SX558 695) East Lowery, Lowery Cottage (SX558 695), Creoby, Lower Steant (SX 555692) Tenement near Lowery and Lowery Farm.

Trying to work out which building is which is difficult. There seems to have been at least three dwellings but only the ruins of two buildings can be seen today. These buildings are all below Lowery Tor (SX 556 698) which is on the slopes of Peek Hill.

There seems to have been a settlement here from around the 1250's. 'Crycebye' was recorded in the Walkhampton Manor Survey and was owned by Michael Slanning, the tenant being Elizabeth Elford in 1585. The size of the property was just 10 acres. It lay in the corner of the parish of Walkhampton where it meets the parish of Meavy near to where the sheds are today in the vicinity of Burrator Lodge. In 1705 John Worth was living at Lowery but the records do not say which building he occupied. On 25th October 1750 a lease was issued to William Smith for 'Crecoble' by the owners Mary Heywood and Araham Elton. On 23rd October 1778 James M. Heywood gave a lease for 99 years to Richard Worth for the same property. Between 1801-1810 there were three properties known as Lowery. The details below come from the Ledgers of Manor of Walkhampton:

1801- 1810 Lower Lowery
John Northmore of Meavy paid 29th Sept. each year

	£	s	d
1 year rent of Lower Lowery	1	1	6
1 year land tax of Lower Lowery	2	-	-
TOTAL:	£3.	1s.	6d.

1801 –1810 Higher Lowery
Richard Worth paid on 29th Sept. each year

	£	s	d
1 year rent of Higher Lowery	-	15	-
1 year land tax of Higher Lowery	2	-	-
TOTAL:	£2.	15s.	0d.

1801-1810 East Lowery
Richard Andrew paid on 29th Sept. each year   £   s   d
1 year rent of East Lowery   -   3   4
1 year rent of West Leathertorr   -   5   10
1 year land tax of West Leathertorr   -   3   -
TOTAL: £0   12s. 2d.

There was no land tax to pay for East Lowery, so this may have just been a small property next to Lower Lowery.

The Church Rate Book of 1834 shows the tenant of Lowery as John Northmore, the rate being 4d. Samuel Hamlyn and Elizabeth (nee Norrish) had moved from Brimpts Farm, Dartmeet to work Middle Lowery Farm the same year and Richard Northmore was at Lowery. In 1840 the Tithe Apportionment for Walkhampton lists, East Lowery, 'Tenement near Lowery', Creboby, Higher Lowery, and Lowery Houses and Courts.

By 1850 Sir Massey Lopes (Maristow) owned Lower Lowery and he took over East Lowery where the tenant was Richard Northmore. Within about 20 years both the East and Lower Lowery were knocked down and replaced by a new, larger farmhouse. Also Maristow built a new barn which still survives today with two incised stones built into it. The stone, of 1873 and with the initials M.L (Massey Lopes), can still be seen in the ruin.

Lower Lowery was then taken over by Samuel Hamlyn from Middle Lowery, whose farmhouse may have fallen into too bad a state of repair to live in. Samuel Hamlyn Jnr's daughter Elizabeth married George Creber from Longstone in 1863. The first reference to Lowery Farm was in 1894 but on 5th April 1897 Mrs Ann Hamlyn and William Henry Hamlyn handed over part of the leasehold of Lowery Farm to the Mayor of Plymouth, so the land could be flooded for the new reservoir. It seems this farm was abandoned in the early 1900's and it may have stood close to Lower Lowery.

Lowery Cottage 1935
(Taken by Sydney Taylor © Dartmoor National Park Authority/ Devon County Council)

Lowery Cottage seems to have been built late in the 1800s and somewhere near Higher Lowery. At one time the Shillibeer family lived in the cottage. Walter German was the Water Engineer at the turn of the 20th century for Plymouth Corporation. His son Len was born in the cottage in July 1928, and his son is David German who used to live in Princetown until a few years ago.

Young George Shillibeer outside Lowery Cottage
(Paul Rendell Collection)

Middleworth (SX572 692)

The earliest known reference to this farm seems to be in 1281 when it was called 'Middelesworthi'. The farmer once again may have been involved in the tin industry for in 1303 Richardus de Middleworthi is recorded coining tin at Ashburton. The Walkhampton Manor Court Rolls for 1789 records the death of William Worth and gives the new tenant as Richard Creft at West Middleworth. In 1801 Joseph Spurr was at East Middleworth and paying £3. 8s. 4d. for rent of this property, Claceywell and Torrland which was somewhere in the Manor of Walkhampton. At West Middleworth there was Richard Creft who paid £2. 15s. for his yearly rent.

By 1840 West Middleworthy was owned by the Maristow Estate and the tenant was Henry Pearse. The Title Apportionment shows some interesting field names including Blue Meadow, Milk Well, Milk Well Moor, and Higher & Lower Moory Meadows. The other dwelling was known simply as Middleworth and was owned by Ralph Lopes (Maristow) and covered 86 acres including 25 fields. It was then decided to build a new farmhouse closer to the track from the original settlement. Tenders were invited for the work and amounted to £71. 10s. 8d. Work started in 1841 and a few years later a barn was also built opposite the farmhouse which still stands today complete with the 'ML 1885' datestone. The new tenant of this newly built farmhouse was John Pengelly, also known as Little John. The last tenant Arthur Williams took over from Little John in 1893 and stayed there until 1914 when Plymouth Corporation took it over. The Williams family then moved to Bickleigh. Towards the end of the 1914-1918 War the Corporation grew potatoes on the land that was once part of Deancombe and Middleworth. There were three soldiers who planted and harvested the crop who lived and kept horses at Middleworth. There was Gaydon the ploughman, Cooper the Carter and Davis the cook. We do not know if they were local men but Davis was a gamekeeper before he joined the army.

By 1919 Middleworth was abandoned. All that remains today are the ruins of the farmhouse and the large granite barn with the datestone on. This survives mainly because the Dartmoor National Park Authority capping the building in the 1970's.

Mullacroft Farm (approx 552 685) and Cottage (552 687)

Where Burrator Lodge now stands was once the site of Mullacroft Farm but little is known about these two dwellings which are both now in ruins. They were on the boundary of three different parishes for many years, Sheepstor, Meavy and Walkhampton; but today they are in the parish of Meavy. This makes it very difficult to trace any documents about Mullacroft. John Creber and Joan Giles married in Walkhampton church in 1686 and went to live at Mullicraft. John Creber was living there in 1718, succeeded by his widow, Joan. The Churchwarden's Records and Accounts in 1723 shows that the farm was liable for payments to Sheepstor Church and they show that Joan Creber lived there until 1731.

In 1840, Mullacroft Farm was marked on the Rendel Railway map as 'A garden & house unoccupied there in'. Rendel Railway was a proposed railway from Plymouth to Exeter, across Dartmoor going through Kingsett Farm and from here towards the Warren House Inn. It was a crazy plan, which never took off – Dartmoor is too hilly.

By 1841, Mullicraft was in the parish of Meavy, and the Tithes Apportionment tells us that Richard Creft was the landowner and the occupier was William Nicholls. It was spelt Mullicroft and the acres were put at just over 30 which included woodlands. Mullacraft Cottage was not marked on the Tithe Map, so must have been built after 1841.

Mullicraft Farm was marked on the 1887 OS 6" map as well as another dwelling, Mullicraft Cottage, beside the road coming down from Yennadon Down.

Henry Creber was a farmer at Lowery before he went to Mullicraft in 1891, meaning the farm we presume. The census for that year tells us that he was aged 32 and was a stonecutters labourer. His wife was Ann and they had two daughters and three sons. There was also a young girl called Eliza Martin who was visiting; she was a Dressmaker who was born in Eggbuckland in Plymouth. Henry Creber died when he was 83 years old and his wife Ann (nee Pengelly) died at 53 years.

A letter was sent to George Creber dated 24th March 1897 from the solicitors and agents for Phillip Cornish and Harry Brooking. It read as follows:

'We hereby give you notice to quit and deliver up on the 25th day of March 1898 the property of the Dwelling house Farm Lands and premises called Mullacraft and woodlands situate in the Parish of Meavy in the County of Devon which you now hold of Philip Alfred Cornish and Harry Brooking'.

Eric Hemery puts Harry Legassick, as the last person to live at Mullicroft Cottage; he was a jobbing-carpenter and a mason. Mullicroft Cottage is now a complete ruin, but only the outline of a cottage and three other outbuildings are still visible in the plantation. The gateway to the courtyard is now blocked up.

Narrator (SX566 688)

This ruined farm can be found at the base of Sheepstor under an outcrop called Narrator, from which the farm took its name. In 1718 there is reference to a property for which John Elford of Longstone paid 4s. for repairs to 'Harris'. This was paid yearly until 1732 when the record in the Churchwarden accounts states 'Harris alias Narrator'. It seems therefore the farm changed it name around this date.

In the Land Tax Assessment of 1780 the farm was called Noretor where the owner-occupier was Walter Willcocks who paid £2.6s.9¼ d. In 1842 the Tithe Apportionment for Sheepstor shows that Narrator was 147 acres with the owner being John Paul. He was farming the area and he was growing apples and potatoes. White's Directory puts John Bayly as Lord of the Manor and he was living at Narrow Tor in 1850.

The Census returns of 1881 puts George Jackman aged 82 years with his wife Elizabeth and son William at Narrator Farm. Sadly in August the following year a tragedy took place there. William Jackman was working on the farm; he was haymaking when a thunderstorm started. As the rain came down, he stuck his pitchfork into a bale of hay and held it over his head to keep him dry. A lighting flash struck the metal prongs which electrocuted him.

John Bayly who owned a lot of property in the village of Sheepstor, was the owner of Narrator Farm in 1908 which comprised of 127 acres of land. Most of this was coarse pasture, with only 8 acres of arable land and just 1 acre being used for timber. By 1914 it was occupied by Fredrick Watkins who was paying rent to the Plymouth Corporation. Five years later Fredrick had handed the farm over to his son Harold and his wife. They had around 100 acres and were paying rent of over £62 per year.

Narrator never became part of Maristow Estate unlike most of the farms in the area and the Watkins stayed there until 1923.

Hilda Watkins feeding the geese at Narrator Farm (Paul Rendell Collection)

They decided to take in holidaymakers during the summer months and some nights it was so busy the family had to sleep in the kitchen by the fire. One visiting family came from Devonport, now part of Plymouth, stayed for two weeks, for several years for their summer holidays. It was a very hard life making a living but nevertheless the family seemed to have enjoyed their life at Narrator. The parish was well-known for its snakes and they would often be found in the farmhouse. One day Harold, who had been working on the farm returned to the farmhouse at midday for a meal. He took off his hat and put in on the sideboard. After his meal he put the hat back on his head and felt something moving about inside. It was an adder! Hilda their daughter used to say there were snakes everywhere. They would come in the kitchen window in their dozens but she was never bitten by one.

During the last few years it was hard making a living at Narrator and they finally left the farm in 1923. They had 22 beasts, 6 horses and colts, 2 pigs, 3 geese, 90 hens and their farm implements which included a farm cart, a spring cart, spring wagon, market trap, a single furrow plough, a granite roller and mowing machine. The family moved to Hellingtown Farm in the centre of Sheepstor village.

The Watkins family in the porch of Narrator Farm 1930's
(Paul Rendell Collection)

Newleycombe (SX 587 699)

Newleycombe farm was in the Newleycombe valley and it was there in 1584 that a 'Survey of Walkhampton' recorded 'John Egbear holds Newlacombe'. Little of the early history remains but between 1801 and 1810 Peter Reed paid a yearly rent of 44s. not a great amount but this was for the building only with an extra 10s. for the land. He also paid rent to the Manor of Walkhampton for Northworthy (Nosworthy Farm). This amounted to £2.15s.0d. for the building and the land. So Newleycombe must have been a very small place. By 1827 it was owned by the Maristow Estate and they valued it as being worth £3.11s.3d. per year. In 1840 the yearly rent was £14.0s.0d. By 1850 Robert Giles was living there and within a few years the farm was abandoned.

Nosworthy (SX 568 694)

First recorded in 1384 when the place was mentioned in a Court Roll. In 1494 John Pyke of Nosworthy was a Jurate at the Stannary Court, which was held at Crocken Tor. The Walkhampton Overseers of the Poor accounts show that in 1701, £2.8s was paid to Edward Atwill who was living at Nosworthy. Peter Reed was living there between 1801 and 1810 but in 1827 Maristow Estates took over the property. Mr Andrew was living there in 1840 and near the farm buildings are two granite stones with dates on. One is on an island in the River Meavy with the date 1840 on it and the other is on a large upright stone behind the buildings with 184[1]. Perhaps 1840 marks a date in the Andrews family's life – death of children for example? In Feb and March 1841 work was being done at Northworthy when new fencing was put up around the island (where the boulder with 1840 is) and trees planted on the island.

In 1850 Sir Massey Lopes of Maristow Estate did major work to the place and soon let it out to Thomas Weslake who stayed until 1883. The church-seating plan for Walkhampton Church had three seats for the family at Nosworthy. In 1891 the farm was still lived in by Thomas and Elizabeth Creber but soon after it was abandoned. As Robert Burnard wrote in his 'Dartmoor Pictorial Records' in 1894: *'abandoned, an ancient structure which will probably soon become a ruin'*. Maristow Estate decided it was uneconomical to run and offered the land to the tenant of nearby Kingset Farm, which they accepted.

Nosworthy Farm 1894
(Robert Burnard –Paul Rendell Collection)

Outholme (SX580 687)

This small farmstead up the Deancombe valley was abandoned over 150 years ago. James Creber was living here in 1741 and the following year he became a Church Warden at Sheepstor where he lived until at least 1757. William Creber was at Outholme in 1779 and a few years later Avis Creber was living there. The Land Tax Assessment records two Outholmes, one tax payable by William and the other by Avis. Were there two dwellings or did they live together and both pay taxes? In 1849 Maristow Estate took over this farm over. George Giles, the Land Steward for the Estate wrote on 6th Feb 1849. 'Another Estate in his hand, Outholme by the death of Richard Creber 4th Feb 1849 age 82, 128 acres. Not very valuable, believed to be for some year's part of £20. It has always been the intended to be laid to Deancomb.' So it seems it was given over to the nearby Deancombe Farm and Outholme was never lived in again. The name Outcombe marked on the maps is modern and was not used at any time while the farm was in use. It seems it had mainly been lived in and worked by the Creber family.

Redstone (SX558 683)

The remains of Redstone are very well covered with trees and brambles. A Mr Redstone, who was a descendant of Richard Redstone, a Churchwarden of Tavistock in 1644, built the farm in the 18th century. In 1844 the owner was John Collier who let John Attwell live there. William Shillabeer was the farmer there in 1866. The last tenant was 32 year old William Brown in 1891. When the reservoir was built he lost a lot of his fields and had a problem making a living. In 1900 he abandoned Redstone or did the Plymouth Corporation push him out?

Riddipit (SX670 700)

There was once a complex of farm buildings here, some of which may have been medieval in origin. The first record of a farm building being here was in 1564 and there was also a tin mill on site which was called Redapit. The land tax for 1784 was £1.13s.0d and was paid by Robert Creber. This was an early property for the Maristow Estate to take over but in the Maristow Rentals it lists Robert Crebar [sic] at the farm paying a yearly rent of £4.6s between 1788 and 1795. The farm was abandoned by 1871 and the enclosures were incorporated with Leather Tor Farm across the valley where Thomas Pearse was the tenant. Remains of the longhouse can still be seen among the brambles and tree stumps.

Roundypark (SX 577 701)

This farm takes its name from the early Bronze Age enclosures which were round in shape. The farm dates from at least 1783 when it was owned by James Modyford and occupied by John Atwill Giles, who was there until 1795. Between 1801 and 1810 Abraham and Robert Giles were paying rent for East Roundypark of 7s. per year. This does not seem a lot of money but they were living at Leathertor Farm at the time where the rent for the property was only 8s; it was the land where the true cost lay. For East Roundypark they paid £1.8s. 0d. while the land for Leathertor was £1.2s.0d. By 1841 Sir Ralph Lopes (Maristow) was the owner and the occupier was Abraham Giles. The farm and land were added to Kingsett Farm in the 1840's but by 1894 the roof had caved in but the stone walls that were built without mortar were still standing.

Stenlake (SX567 709)

This is one of the oldest farms within the area. First reference is in 1281 'Richard de la Stentlake' being the owner of a dwelling here. There is a small stream nearby called Stenlake, so did Richard take his name from this stream? The word 'lake' on Dartmoor is another term for a stream or brook. In the 1700's there were four farmsteads here, Lower, Higher, West and Middle Stenlake. The ruined buildings we see today were built in the early 1800s. There was an East and West Stenlake in the 1840s. By the early 20th Century only one of these farms remained and Mr & Mrs Gill lived there. They had their supplies delivered by Frank Hodge who worked at Bolt's Store in Princetown. When he arrived at the farm there was always apple pie and scrumpy waiting for him. The last occupant left Stenlake in the early 1920's. The roof was still intact until the 1960's when after a dry summer it fell in. Throughout the life of this settlement it was always called Stenlake, but today it is marked on the OS map as Stanlake and this is a mistake by the map makers.

Stenlake Farm
(Taken by Sydney Taylor © Dartmoor National Park Authority/ Devon County Council)

Vinneylake (SX562 693)

First reference to this farm was in the Walkhampton Manor Survey 1585 when John Shellabere was one of the tenants of the Vennalake tenements. Vinneylake was home to the Pearse family from 1673 until 1838 when Richard Pearse gave up the lease. There are not many families within the area that can claim such a long lease of a farm, 165 years. John & Grace Pearse were living on one of two farms here, Higher or Lower, while their son Richard was living in the other one in the early 1830's. John died in 1836 and Grace died aged 92 two years later on 19th October 1838, after which Maristow Estate took over one of two tenements at Vinneylake. The Pearses had leased their property from the Walkhampton Manor but the lease had now run out. Their son Richard Pearse was paying an annual rent of £20 for his farm and Maristow felt that his parents' property was probably worth the same and Richard then took over both farms but not for very long.

Within weeks he had upset his new landowner, for he was cutting down thorns and trees in the woods adjoining Nosworthy Bridge and a letter was sent to him asking him to stop as it was not in the Agreement which was signed by him on 28th Oct 1838.

Next year there was a different tenant at Vinneylake; perhaps Richard Pearse was not a very good tenant and was kicked out. This kind of thing often happened and Maristow would kick out an unsatisfactory tenant the following year. The new person at the farm was Isaac Stancombe from Widecombe. George Giles representing Maristow had for months been looking for a new tenant for Vinneylake. It seems that Isaac Stancombe had asked before to move there but he was turned down. He had lost his wife a little earlier and was looking for a smaller farm for himself, his two daughters and his son but George Giles told him in a letter dated 28th Oct 1839 '...I cannot..lett to you the Farm at Vinneylake.' But oddly, within a few weeks Isaac was living at the farmhouse and his name is listed in the Tithe Apportionment of the same year. Both Higher and Lower Vinneylake were listed as two houses but had been farmed as one for many years but under two different leases. In 1866 John Hamlyn was living there and stayed until 1910. When the reservoir was being built a few years earlier he lost some of the lower fields but the farm was still being worked.

Vinneylake Farm with Leather Tor behind (Paul Rendell Collection)

In 1871 Thomas Pearse, who was born at Vinneylake and then living at Leathertor Farm, was in court giving a statement about problems to do with the hatch (sluiced gate) on the Plymouth Leat at Headweir. He stated he had lived at Vinneylake for 25 years. George Hamlyn afterwards took over until 1926 when the new roads were built around Burrator Reservoir.

OTHER BUILDINGS

Ball Cottage

This building can no longer be seen as it was pulled down in December 1849. It stood near the main car park at Nosworthy Bridge, on private land. Between 1830 and 1838 a Nicholas Stephens lived here. At this time the property was described in Walkhampton Manor Rental as a 'House, Norsworthy Ball'. Between 1847-1849 John Ruby paid the rent of £2 12s per year. In 1849 he decided to give up his cottage and it was pulled down; the garden and the land then became part of Middleworth. The cottage may at one time have been part of Bal Mine, a small tin mine situated where the large car park is today. There are the remains of a wheel pit and leat to the north of the car park. Please note there is nothing to see of Ball Cottage and it is on private land.

Burrator Lodge (SX551 685)

The Lodge was built in 1895 by Plymouth Corporation for the Water Engineer to live in as a replacement for Head Weir Cottage. Amos Shillibeer lived there until 1898 when his son who was the Forman of the newly completed Burrator Reservoir took over. Burrator Lodge was lived in by various members of the Shillibeer family until 1940. The last Water Engineer to live at the Lodge was Gerrard Taylor. Today Burrator Lodge is used by South West Lakes Trust and is private property so please do not trespass.

Burrator Lodge 2006 (Paul Rendell)

Head Weir Cottage

The Plymouth Corporation built Headweir Cottage in 1871 but it stood for less than 27 years. It was built for the Plymouth Leat Forman, Amos Shillibeer and his wife. Amos's duty was to look after the leat from Headweir to Jump (now known as Roborough on the edge of Plymouth). Amos was the third generation of his family to be responsible for the upkeep of the Plymouth Leat.

In 1891 it was a very bad year for maintaining the water supply to Plymouth. A severe blizzard struck the area on 9th March and the leat froze over. On 11th March of that year Mr Bellamy, the Borough Surveyor took all available Corporation staff from Plymouth and they went to Headweir, their job was to clear the leat of snow and ice. It was an impossible task for the number of staff involved. The Mayor, Mr T.T. Bond engaged a local contractor to help keep the leat from freezing over but the 100 men now at work still could not keep the water flowing. The Mayor appealed for more help and the military responded with 100 marines and 200 soldiers. The men worked all night and the next day until the train got through from Plymouth bringing more troops so they could be relieved. They formed gangs and spread out along the leat, which in places was lying under twelve feet of frozen snow. Headweir Cottage also had to be cleared of snow. They won in the end but it took over 600 men to do it. This episode was the last straw for the Corporation, as plans were already underway to build a reservoir and pipe the water to Plymouth.

Headweir Cottage was knocked down in 1894 and the foundation tablet taken away to be later placed in the grounds of Burrator Lodge. It read: '1871 R.C. Serpell Mayor Plymouth Corporation Waterworks. James King Chairman'. In 1898 the remains of the cottage disappeared beneath the water of the reservoir.

Longstone Manor (SX557 685)

The original building is thought to have been built in the mid 13th century. It is also believed that the Herbert family may have built it. It is known that in 1483 John Scudamore, the Lord of Sheepstor only had two daughters, Johanne and Dionisia. John Elford from Peter Tavy met and married Johanne and thus he became the Lord of the Manor after John Scudamore died in 1517 and that is how the Elford family became involved in the small parish of Sheepstor. The Elfords prospered and many alterations took place over the years until 1633 when a new house was built for Walter and Barbara Elford. After some further changes this is the house we see today. By 1637 John Elford was living here and was known as John of the Windstrew because he built the windstrew – a threshing platform in the grounds.

The Elfords invested in tin mining and had shares in many of the local mines. They also had a tinner's mill which is now under the reservoir. In 1705 another John Elford owned shares in 'Great Evill' which could be Evil Combe in the Plym Valley. He also had shares in 'Lonston Beam', Rattlebrook (Lydford), North Amacombe Ridge (Lydford), Broomparks (Hoo Meavy) and in 'Great Rowter', on the slopes of Rough Tor, not far from Longstone. John married Admonition, daughter of John Prideaux of Prideaux Place in Cornwall.

On 29th December 1741 John Commins, who was an apprentice to John Elford, ran away from Longstone with four years still to serve. The local paper reported this a month later together with a description: *"Apprentice was aged 20; he was five feet high, slender with lank brown hair, thin face and ruddy countenance. He was wearing a new pair of shoes and stockings, dark stripped coarse woollen waistcoat, white kersey coat and breeches, and a dark coarse shag riding coat with bone buttons."* It is not known if he was ever returned but the question is why did he leave?

The Elfords were the only family to occupy Longstone Manor and the last one died on 29th November 1755. All his six children had died before him. The Manorial status of Longstone now changed from a grand house to a farmstead. Some of the buildings were converted into pig-stys, stables and cow sheds, thus accounting for the good granite dressings to be found in these buildings today. In the Land Tax Assessment for 1780 Thomas Amies was the owner-occupier and paid tax amounting to £.1s. 4d. By 1820 the property was owned by Sir Ralph Lopes (Maristow Estate) and from 1841 to 1850 it was leased to William Nichols.

The last tenants of the farm were John and Elizabeth Norrish Creber who moved there in 1851 and lived there until the reservoir was built. One of their sons George married Annie Elizabeth from Lowery, across the valley in 1863. In 1881 John was 78 years old, his wife was 70 and they had four children and a servant, William Willcocks age 16. On 2nd May 1888 John Creber died leaving the sum of £873 in his estate which was given to his widow. Longstone was never lived in again. The roof of the building was taken off and the date stone, which was inscribed 1633 WEB (Walter Elford Barbara), removed for safe keeping to the the newly built Burrator Lodge when the farm was abandoned in 1898. Plymouth Corporation planted the area around Longstone with conifers in 1921.

Today Longstone stands beside the reservoir and it is hard to imagine how grand this building would have been in its heyday with its lovely gardens etc. The water for the Manor House was via a leat from the River Plym many miles away. There used to be a number of orchards beside the house as well as a cider house and the windstrew previously referred to which can still be seen among the trees. Several water troughs were brought from other farms when the valley was flooded. The main walls of the old Georgian house still stand with a fine front entrance and two fireplaces with huge granite blocks for the lintels. You can still see part of the old road starting beside the Manor House (the old road normally under water) leading to Sheepstor Bridge (also under water). Dartmoor National Park Authority has recently capped the ruins.

Longstone takes its name from a menhir, a Bronze Age standing stone which can still be seen today when the water in the reservoir is low. The Longstone is about five feet high and was last used as a gatepost.

Park Cottage Inn (SX559 679)

Two cottages were built in the 1840's on the outskirts of Sheepstor village. Sheepstor did not have an inn at this time and with the building of Burrator Reservoir being suggested in the mid 1890's it was decided to turn the cottages into a pub. It was intended to serve ale to the many hundreds of men who would be working and living nearby. For 30 years the eight-roomed inn was in the hands of Josias Nelder. The water supply was taken off the old Longstone Leat, which originally brought water from the River Plym to the Longstone Manor. Plymouth Corporation issued an indenture on 5th May 1924 to buy the inn which they closed down six years later saying it was unsafe due to drainage problems. The 'drainage problems' were in fact the waste from the inn itself which was polluting the reservoir and this had to stop. It was soon knocked down by the Corporation and today the site is used as a car park with little trace of any building.

*Building Sheepstor Dam with Park Cottage Inn behind 1895
(Plymouth and West Devon Record Office)*

OTHER INTERESTING ITEMS

Classeywell Cross

This granite cross was on the old route used by monks going between Buckfast and Tavistock/Buckland abbeys. In 1902 the cross was in a very poor state with only the head remaining; according to William Crossing, it was found beside Classeywell Pool. The cross was re-erected and a new shaft added in 1915 by the Reverend H. Hugh Breton but in all likelihood not in the original spot. It is believed to have been lower down the hillside initially. Today the cross is known as Crazywell.

Classeywell Pool

This large man made pool was built as a reservoir by the tin miners. Around the upper rim there are the signs of old leats which could have been used to bring in water to the reservoir. This water would have been taken to workings lower down the Newleycombe valley via the stream and gully we see there today.

Many local people used to believe that the water in the pool rose and fell with the tide in Plymouth Sound. The pool was thought to be bottomless and the good folks of the parish are said to have tied all the bell ropes of Walkhampton Church together and let them into the pool without reaching the bottom. There is a another legend that if you look into the pool at midnight on Midsummer's Eve you will see the image of the next person who will die within the parish. In the 1970s two friends of the author were drinking in the Royal Oak pub at Meavy and were told this story by some of the locals. Being young they scoffed at the old men and said they were off to find out if it was true. Soon they were on their motorbike on their way to the pool, arriving just before midnight. The next day on the radio there was a report about an accident where a motorbike had taken a bend near Yelverton too fast and gone through the hedge, killing two people instantly. Had they been drinking too much or was the legend true? The author was at the pool one Midsummer's Eve in the 1990s but was gone again by the time the chimes struck twelve.

Devonport Leat

This watercourse used to carry over 2 millions gallons (4.5 million litres) of fresh water daily to the town of Devonport and its Dockyard. The Dockyard used to be called Plymouth Dock or sometimes just 'Dock' and the water course was 'Dock Leat'. In 1824 Plymouth Dock was renamed Devonport. This leat takes water from the West Dart River just above Wistman's Wood, and from the River Cowsic and the Blackabrook. The contract for its construction was awarded in 1793 to Thomas Gray from Exeter but by 1797 very little work had been done and a second contractor, the Plymouth Dock Waterworks, was called in to help. The project was completed by the end of 1801. Today the water flows for 17 miles and enters Burrator Reservoir near Burrator Lodge, thus still supplying fresh water to Devonport and the Dockyard.

Princetown Railway and Burrator Halt

The first Princetown Railway was a horse-drawn tramway from Crabtree, Plymouth to the granite quarries on Walkhampton Common and the first rails were put down in 1823. It was in 1883 that steam engines began hauling trains on the newly constructed branch line from Yelverton, laid mostly on the bed of the old tramway. It took ten and half miles by rail to get around the rugged tors from Yelverton to Princetown, yet it is only six miles by road. The line closed in March 1956.

Near Burrator Dam, high above the road is the old railway line and the remains of Burrator Halt. Popular belief is that the Burrator and Sheepstor Halt (to give it its full name) was built for visitors and walkers from Plymouth. However that was not the main reason for the building of the railway halt. On 13th January 1924, Plymouth Corporation Water Committee was informed that the Great Western Railway Company was preparing to erect a platform on Yennadon Down in connection with the conveyance of workmen to and from Plymouth.

Work had started on 17th December the previous year on enlarging Burrator Reservoir. There were about 200 men engaged in raising both Burrator and Sheepstor Dams. Huts were brought in to provide sleeping accommodation for the workers but a lot of men were travelling from

Plymouth daily to the site. Until now these men had to get off the train at Dousland and walk the rest of the way.

From the end of January 1924, the men were issued at the end of each working day with a railway permit which allowed them a return ticket for the following day from any one of three stations in Plymouth - Millbay, North Road and Mutley. Each man's name was to be written in a book and his number put on the back of the ticket.

It was over a year later, on 4th February 1925 that the Burrator Halt was made available for workmen only, but from 18th May the same year, the halt was opened to the public. The platform was built of heavy timbers supported upon trestle legs with cross members. Concrete posts carrying a steel rail and several steel wires formed the back. A wooden name panel bore the cast iron lettering 'Burrator and Sheepstor'. At the southern end of the platform was the waiting room. It was a timber building on a concrete base with two small windows. Sadly only the two kissing gates and steps that lead to the Halt remains today.

(Paul Rendell Collection)

EXPLORING THE AREA

The walks have been arranged to include as many items of interest as possible which were mentioned in the preceding chapters. The ground can be muddy after heavy rain, some of the routes are on open moorland and in parts are rough under foot with loose stones. Please wear walking boots and be prepared for 'Dartmoor' weather which can mean any weather at any time of the year. The taking of compass bearings will not be necessary for these walks, but take a compass and map with you in case you wander off the route. If you want to learn how to use a map & compass contact Dartmoor National Park Authority (01822 890414) or Dartmoor Search & Rescue Team (Plymouth) (01752 518669). Both offer courses on navigation.

STARTING PLACE: Nosworthy Bridge (SX 569 692) which is at the far end of Burrator Reservoir. There are two car parks here. The walks start at the bridge.

AMENITIES: Toilets (normally closed during the winter) at Burrator Dam. Ice cream van sometimes at Nosworthy Bridge and at Burrator Dam. Shops and pubs at Yelverton. Pub at Meavy.

RECOMMENDED MAP: You should not attempt to do these walks without taking a map. Ordnance Survey Explorer OL28 Dartmoor. South Sheet.

WARNING: There are old mine workings as well as ruined buildings which can be very dangerous so take care when exploring.

EXPLORING THE BURRATOR AREA

"Reproduced from 1954 Ordnance Survey map with kind permission of the Ordnance Survey"

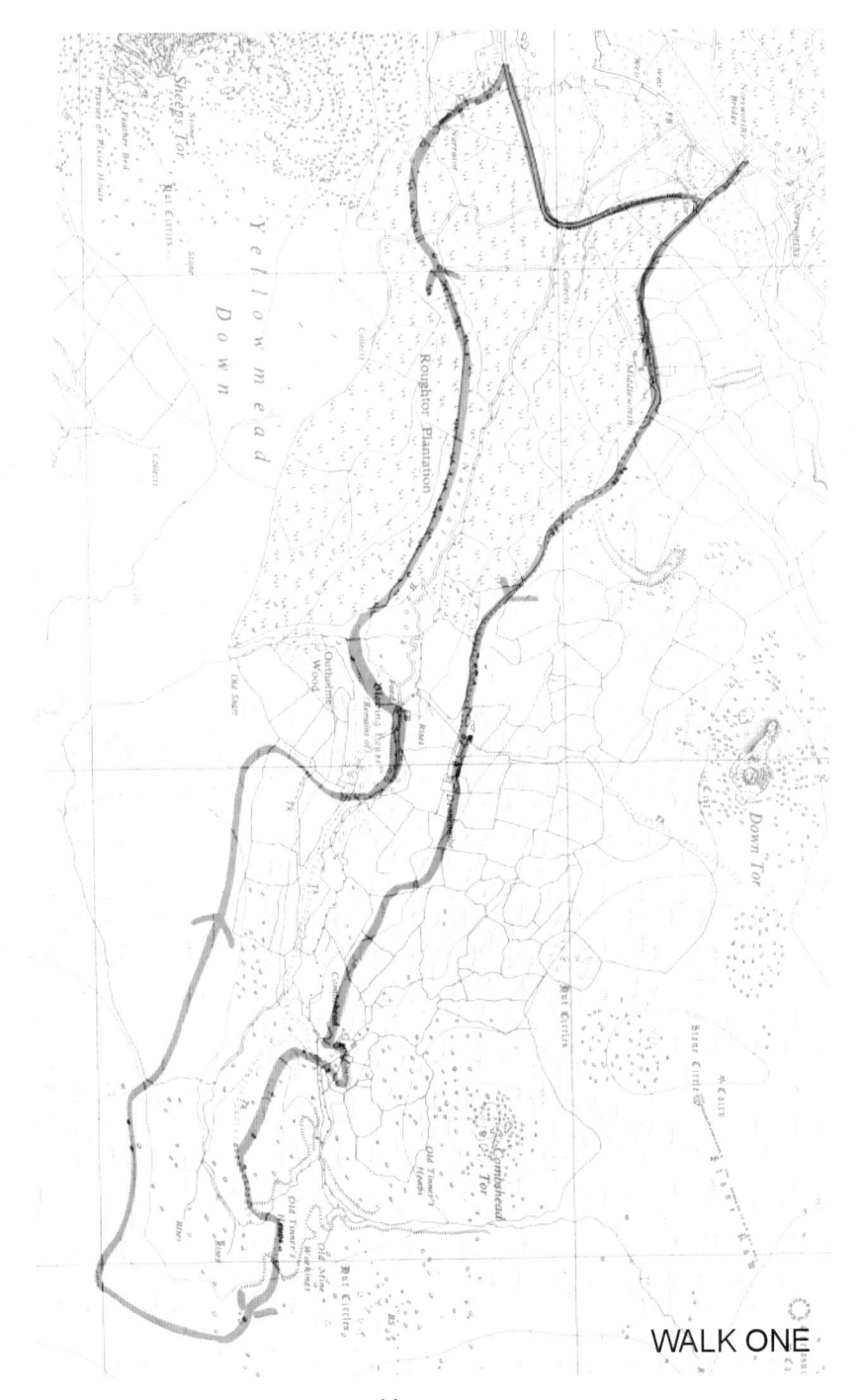

WALK ONE

EXPLORING THE BURRATOR AREA

WALK ONE

BASIC ROUTE: Nosworthy Bridge – Deancombe Farm – Combeshead Farm – Eylesbarrow Mine – Narrator Brook – Outcome- Narrator Farm.

DISTANCE: About 6 miles.

TERRAIN: Track, fields, moorland and tracks through woods.

From Nosworthy Bridge take the road to the larger car park. This used to be the site of Bal Mine, a tin mine. The wheel pit beside the car park can still be seen as well as the leat leading to it. **Now follow the track ahead of you uphill. It soon levels out and you will come to a ruined building on the right.** This was the barn at Middleworth Farm. This building used to have two floors with animals on the ground floor and hay above. The old farm-house was where the woods are now; later it was rebuilt to the right of the barn beside the track. All that is left today are just a few walls of the farmhouse.

Carry on along the track and when you come out into the open you will see a large tor on the left. This is Down Tor. Continue along the track until you come to some more ruined farm buildings on the left. This was Deancombe Farm from 1566 until about 1850 when there were two farms here – East and West Deancombe. The more modern buildings can be found further along the track and on the right hand side. There are several buildings and other items to be seen here including a small raised garden and the hayrick with some of the staddle stones still in place. The small stream that intersects the track between the two farms comes from the adit of a tin mine (a drainage channel dug into the hillside).It seems the soil was very poor within the area so the farmers also worked for tin. The remains can be seen in and around the fields. The old lane leading up the hill from the two farms was the way the farmers drove their stock onto the open moor below Down Tor.

EXPLORING THE BURRATOR AREA

Continue through the fields. Where the track forks take the left hand one heading towards the big rock on the skyline. This is known as Cuckoo Rock because the farmer at Combeshead heard his first cuckoo every year from the top of that rock.

Go through the fields belonging to Deancombe Farm, cross the boggy area via the stepping stones and head for the holly tree below Cuckoo Rock. Before you reach the tree turn right and head down towards the stone wall, go through the gap in the wall. Bear left and head towards the gateway and cross another field via the track. In 1985 there was a major battle here when American and British forces fought it out. It was the setting for 'Revolution' a major film based on the American War of Independence starring Donald Sutherland, Al Pacino, Nastassja Kinski and Annie Lennox (of pop group Eurythmics fame). The film critics were scathing with comments like 'great scenery, shame about the acting' etc. and the film was a flop. The film company lost millions of pounds.

Keep going across the fields and through the 2nd gateway, fork left along the grassy track to a ruined wall, with a gate post beyond. Cross over the wall and you will see the ruins of Combeshead Farm on your right. This was the last farm to be abandoned around Burrator in 1931. The building on the left was an animal shed and the small building was the outside toilet. The farm house was further along on the right.

Carry on past the gate post and go up a grassy path (over grown in the summer months by bracken). This leads to a Potato Cave where the farmer would store his 'roots' for the winter. Swedes and potatoes were laid on straw or dried bracken and covered with the same. There would have been a metal gate across the entrance. There are a number of potato caves, beehive huts and stores in the area which would have been used to store tin, tools, crops and maybe used to manufacture some of the 'hard stuff'. Remember it was hard living in this wild place and a drop of cider, ale or something stronger was something to look forward to.

EXPLORING THE BURRATOR AREA

Now take the path opposite the cave which goes down the hill to Combeshead Brook and cross over by the ford, or if you go down stream a few yards you can cross over what is known as a 'clapper bridge' (stone bridge). Follow the track to the right and immediately bear left following the small path leading up through the large rocks and head to the top passing some old mining pits and a cluster of trees. Once on top, cross level ground and head towards the large mounds you see on the skyline ahead before dipping into an ancient tin streaming area.

It is believed this place was being worked for tin in the 1100s. You can see there was once a lot of activity here. The big tor on the left is Combeshead Tor. **Follow the track through the workings and head for the far bank with a small area of reeds visible on the side of the hill. Walk up the hill with the reeds to your right. This patch of reeds is very boggy as a result of water coming from Two Brothers Adit. Here you will find a small hole in a gully with water coming out of the hillside; it is part of Eylesbarrow Tin Mine which was worked between 1814 and 1852.**

Walk around the head of the adit which was once named North Adit, later called Two brothers Adit. Nearby is a big pit. This used to be a mine shaft and in later years a 50 foot diameter waterwheel was placed in it and used to transmit power to the working area higher up the hillside. There are two metal rings nearby fixed to a rock; these were used to tie the water wheel down. Higher up the hillside and to the East there are many buildings and workings associated with tin mining.

Now go south to where there is a boundary stone on the skyline. You will see another boundary stone on the left (uphill) but head for the one straight on. It has PCWW on it which stands for Plymouth Corporation Water Works and was put up to mark the boundary of the land around Burrator Reservoir belonging to the Corporation. There are some great views from here: to the right Combeshead Tor, North Hessary Mast at Princetown and the Deancombe valley below.

EXPLORING THE BURRATOR AREA

Now head downhill (north west) towards the plantation to the right of Sheepstor. Carry on this line until you reach a gully and turn right down the gully towards a lone tree above a deep gully. Follow track left above the gully, crossing a bank/wall and head towards the two trees you will see and soon you will reach a stone wall on the right with trees on and beside it. Follow this until you reach another wall with a fence in front of it. Turn right and go along the fence downhill towards Narrator Brook. Cross the fence by the stile signposted Deancombe and continue down into the woods. To your left are the remains of a tinner's mill. This is where the tin was worked during the 16th century.

Continue beside the brook until a wide track appears in front of you. Cross another stile and turn left towards Sheepstor Common (signposted) and just before the track goes up a steep part of the hill there is a gate and a stile on your right. Cross over and follow the path, cross the stream and join a wider track. Now turn right and go through the woods. Do not go over the stile by itself on the right but carry on until you reach a gate and a stile together. Go over the stile and continue along the track until it turns right through a gateway and into the courtyard of Narrator Farm. There is very little left of this farm. The farmhouse was to the right and the out-buildings were to the left.

Carry on down to the road, turn right and follow it back to Norsworthy Bridge. Be careful on the road it can be busy during the summer and at weekends. Keep to the right hand side, facing the traffic.

EXPLORING THE BURRATOR AREA

WALK TWO

BASIC ROUTE: Nosworthy Bridge – Kingsett Farm – Crazywell Pool – Devonport Leat – Stanlake – Leathertor Farm.

DISTANCE: About 6 miles

TERRAIN: Tracks, fields, moorland, beside leat and through woodlands via a track.

From Nosworthy Bridge take the track from the tarmac road and head uphill to where it forks. This was the site of Nosworthy Farm, but now there are just a few low walls remaining of what was once a large farm. **Take the right hand track uphill with the woods on the left.** These trees were planted after the reservoir was completed. In front of you is Down Tor across the valley.

Continue along the track until you see a tree on the field boundary wall on the right which turns sharply away from you. Leave the track and bear right across the moorland to the corner of a wall on the left. Go through the gap in the wall keeping this wall to your left go through the gate into the field and cross the gully. This was once Keaglesborough Tin Mine, believed to date back to the 1500's. **Keep following the grassy track and head towards the tall beech tree before you. Go through the gate to the ruined buildings of Kingsett Farm.** The beech tree was planted in the 1880s by the Pease family. The building on the right was last used as a shippon with a cart shed beside it.

After exploring the farm, make for the fir tree you can see, bear right keeping the stone wall to your right and cross over two low walls. Looking back you will see Kingsett in its beautiful setting with Burrator Reservoir behind.

Continue on through the fields and over another low wall. Soon the wall you are following will join another wall at right angles to it. Go through the gap and follow the grassy track for a few yards until

EXPLORING THE BURRATOR AREA

you come to a large pointed rock in a field. **From here look left and head towards the cross on the skyline. Soon you will reach two gateposts. Go through them and you are at Classey Farm.** Today the farm, the nearby cross and the pool are all called Crazywell. This must have been a very small farm as it was part of Kingsett in the early 20th Century. **Now make for the cross on the skyline and on reaching the stony track turn right.** This track was once the principal access to the five farms within this valley. Norsworthy, Kingsett, Roundypark, Classey and Newlewycombe. It was also used by miners bringing tin out of the valley. Today the track leads only to Peat Cott and Whiteworks.

Further along the track you cross a small stream where you should fork left and up hill towards the cross. At Classiwell Cross turn left towards Leather Tor and Sharpitor in the direction of Classiwell Pool. Do not linger too long at this pool in case you see a reflection of yourself. The story goes if you see a reflection of yourself in the pool you will die within the year! If the pool is full of water this means it is high tide in Plymouth and if the water is low then the tide is out. All this is according to folklore of course.

Classeywell (Crazy Well) Cross with Burrator Reservoir behind.
(Pauline Greenwood)

EXPLORING THE BURRATOR AREA

WALK TWO

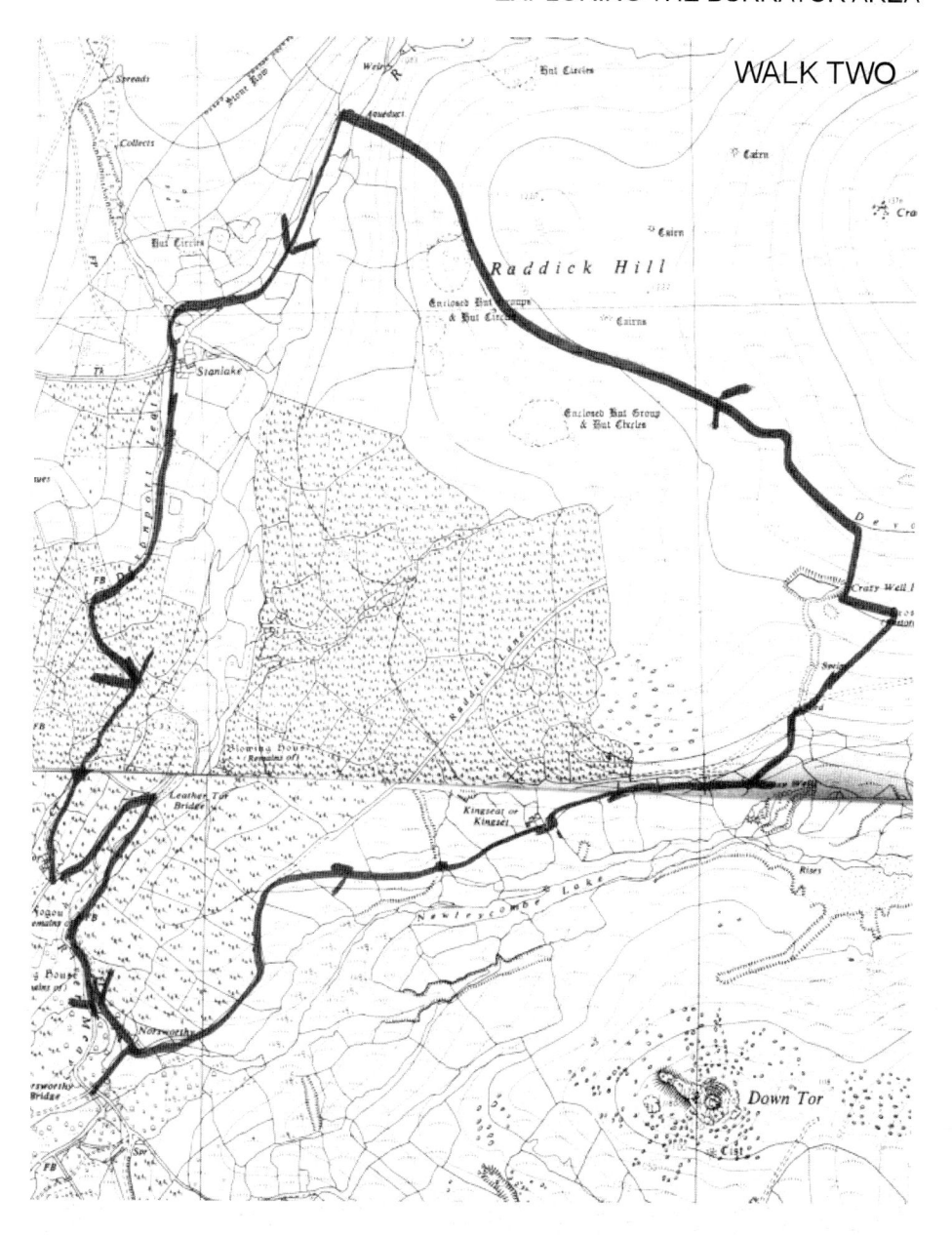

"Reproduced from 1954 Ordnance Survey map with kind permission of the Ordnance Survey"

EXPLORING THE BURRATOR AREA

When you reach the pool turn right and head uphill until you reach the Devonport Leat and turn left follow the flow. Cross over the leat by means of one of the several bridges along this section. The flow of water increases rapidly as it goes down hill. Beware of the clitter (loose stones) at this point. You will soon see the leat again in the valley below going towards the trees. As you come down this steep hill you will cross a dry leat bed passing from right to left. This was the Keaglesborough Mine leat. This mine was near Kingsett Farm. **At the bottom of the hill is a small quarry to your right which is where the stone was taken from to build the 1792 aqueduct known as 'Iron Bridge'.** The aqueduct carries the leat over the River Meavy and beside the river you can see the remains of tin streaming.

Still following the leat until you reach the plantation and here you will see on the left the ruins of Stenlake Farm. This was once a large settlement with two farms. They were abandoned in the 1920s and although the 19th century farmhouse was still standing with a roof in 1935, by 1967 when R. G. Haynes surveyed the site, the building had been demolished.

Now cross the stile and continue alongside the leat. The tor on the left which you will be able to see from the clearing is Sheepstor. In front is Leathertor and to the right is Sharpitor.

When you reach the 2nd clapper bridge turn left down a track until you reach some more ruined buildings on both sides of the track. This was Leathertor Farm which once comprised two farmsteads. Cross the stile and turn left. After about 50 yards you will see a big cave on the left. This was a Potato Cave where the farmer at the nearby farm used to keep his root crops including swedes as well as potatoes. This cave goes back a long way and used to have an iron gate across the entrance.

EXPLORING THE BURRATOR AREA

Leather Tor Farm Potato Cave
(Paul Rendell)

Carry on along the track to Leather Tor Bridge and cross it. This 19th century bridge is a wonderful example of a clapper with block parapet walls. It replaced the older and smaller bridge a little way up-stream, the pillars of which can be seen on the bank. In the Walkhampton Vestry Minutes book it states that on 20th June 1855 the Parishoners decided to build a bridge at Redipit Steps. This is the name of the ford beside the bridge. It was built in the summer of 1855 at a cost of £26 10s and Walkhampton Manor contributed £10 towards it. The builders were William Mashford and George Worth who constructed the bridge to a the very high standard required for the benefit of the many farmers within this area who had horses and carts and needed to cross the ford at this point. Today the bridge is a Grade II listed structure.

Now turn right and follow the track back to the ruins of Nosworthy Farm. Turn right at the junction of track and you will soon be back at your start point.

APPENDIX: TENANTS OF FARMS

NAME OF FARM: **Combeshead**
FIRST RECORDED: Pre 1768
SOME TENANTS: John Geels (1762); John Giles (1768); William Creber (1768); William Creber (1780); Avis Creber (1781-1795); James Creber (1801-1810); William Creber (1803); John Harvey (1866); George Pengelly (1880); William Pengelly (1920's)
LAST USED: December 1931

NAME OF FARM: **Classeywell**
FIRST RECORDED: 1575
SOME TENANTS: Nicholas Bonsal (1575-1585); Elias Giles & Robert Ceber (1780); William Giles (1765-1781); Joseph Spurr (1791); John Pearse (1824); John Spurr (1833); John Gregory (1825-1850); John Giles (1866)
LAST USED: Between 1910-1914

NAME OF FARM: **Deancombe (East & West)**
FIRST RECORDED: 1567
SOME TENANTS: Alice Winditt (1567-1585); Robert Cockle (W 1585); Robert Toop (E 1673); Ann Barter (W 1762); Roger Atwill (1765-1784); William Creber (W 1776); Elias Giles (1780); Oliver Atwill (1781); Robert Atwill (E 1782); Elias Giles (1784); Avis Creber (1784); John King (W 1801-1810); William Creber (1803-1810); Henry Pearse (1820); John Northmore (E&W 1820-1835); Richard Creber (1821); Richard Andrew (1835-1838); Thomas Fairweather & Henry Broadbridge (1841); John Creber (1842); Richard Andrew (E 1825-1838); John Peek (E 1836); Richard Andrew (E 1838); Thomas Fairweather & Richard Bradridge (W 1839).
LAST USED: Between 1910-1914

NAME OF FARM: **Essworthy**
FIRST RECORDED: 1718
SOME TENANTS: Sarah Creber (1718), Phillip William & John Bounsall (1746), William Bounsall (1750), John Boundsall (1763), Robert Andrew (1770), George Shillibeer (1789), William Nichols (1793), George Shillibeer (1794), William Cann (1800), Henry Luscombe (1812), John Bidlake (1829) John Hook (1842) Richard Creft (1844-1846), John Luscombe (1850), Joseph Lampin (1851), William Spear (1856), Richard Creber (1861), William Clifton (1865-1868) William Cann (1880), George Creber (1897-1898)
LAST USED: 1898

EXPLORING THE BURRATOR AREA

NAME OF FARM: **Kingsett (East & West)**
FIRST RECORDED: 1333
SOME TENANTS: John Adams (1584-1585), John Egbear (1585), Phillip Cockle (1662-1666), Phillip Cockle (E&W 1673), Ralph Cockell (1702-1727), John Giles (1738), Mary Staddon (1765-1776), Richard Ward (1776), John More Knighton (two Kingsetts 1776-1810), Mary Knighton (two Kingsetts 1817-1846), James Henry Deacon (1839), Grace Hancock (1847), Richard Worth (1849), John Pearse (1881- 1917), Sam Pearse (1917-1924).
LAST USED: 1924

NAME OF FARM: **Leathertor (East & Middle, West)**
FIRST RECORDED: 1511 (maybe earlier)
SOME TENANTS: William & Jane Dunster (1511), John Browne (1523), William Elford (W 1565-1585), John Dunterfield (1565-1585), John Wedlake (1673), John Shellabeare & Nicholas Worth (1673), Nicholas & Michael Worth (1700), William Creber (1716-1738), Walter Crossman (W 1717), Robert Worth (1743-1784), John Atwill Giles(1784-1785), Abraham & Robert Giles (1801-1810), Abraham Giles (E&W 1811-1842), Abraham Giles (E & M 1825-1826), George Andrew (W 1825-1831), Richard Northmore (W 1832), Samuel Hamlyn (W 1832-1839), Thomas Pearse (1881-1890), John Lillicrapp (1890-1924).
LAST USED: 1924

NAME OF FARM: **Lowery**
(Lower, Higher, Cottage, Lowery Stent, tenement nr. Lowery)
FIRST RECORDED: 1479
SOME TENANTS: John Houghe (1479), Philip Pyke (1479-1510), Richard Elford (1511), Isota Turner (151550-1585), Joan Shalabere (E 1562-1585), Stephen Knight (L 1665), Walter Crossman (1715), John Shelluber (L 1730), Richard Worth (1751-1778), Richard Northmore (1758), John Northmore (L 1801-1831), Richard Worth (H 1801-1820), Richard Andrew (E 1801-1810), Plymouth Dock Water Co (Cottage & Lowery Stent 1807-1836), Ann Worth (H 1911-1848), Thomas Tatam (E 1811-1820), John Northworthy (1820-1823), George Andrew (H 1823), William Norrish (L 1825-1826), George Andrew, (H 1825-1831), Richard Northmore (E & H 1832), Samuel Hamlyn (L 1839), John Giles (Tenement nr 1841), Samuel Hamlyn (H 1841),
LAST USED: ---

Burrator Reservoir just after completion. (Paul Rendell Collection)

Steam Crane at Burrator Dam 1895 (Courtesy Paul London)

Workmen at the Burrator trench Feb 1896 (Courtesy Paul London)

laying pipes in the Plymouth Leat near Dousland 1930's. (Courtesy Paul London)

Sheepstor School 1920. Many of the children in this photograph came from the Burrator Farms. The father of the girl third from the right in the front row used to run Park Cottage Inn. (Paul Rendell Collection)

*Ruins of Longstone House 1930's.
(Taken by Sydney Taylor © Dartmoor National Park / Devon County Council)*

BIBLIOGRAPHY

Brown, Mike (1995)   The Gazetteer of Dartmoor Names. *Forest Publishing.*
Brown, Mike (1997)   Sheepstor - owners & occupiers list 1718-1914. *Dartmoor Press.*
Brown, Mike (1998)   Walkhamton's Abandoned Farms Vol 1-9. *Dartmoor Press.*
Brown, Mike (2001)   Walkhampton Parish History. *Internet site only.*
Crossing, William (1902)   The Ancient Stone Crosses of Dartmoor.
Burnard, Robert (1894)   Dartmoor Pictorial Records. *Published Privately.*
Edmondson, Elizabeth & Taylor, Rosemary. (1993) The Creber Connexion. *Published Privately.*
Elford, Laura (1976)   The Elfords; the story of an ancient English family. *Published Privately.*
Gerrard, Sandy (1996)   Meavy Valley Archaeology. Site Report no 2. *Published Privately.*
Hawkings, David. J (1987) Water From the Moor. *Devon Books.*
Hamilton-Leggett, P (1994)   The Manor of Walkhampton 1585. *Published Privately.*
Hemery, Eric (1983)   High Dartmoor. *Robert Hale Ltd.*
Hemery, Eric (1986)   Walking the Dartmoor Waterways. *David & Charles.*
Hemery, Pauline (1999)   The Book of Meavy. *Halsgrove.*
James, Trevor (2004)   Bodies on the Moor. *Orchard Publications.*
Kingdom, R, Anthony (1991)   The Yelverton to Princetown Railway. *Forest Publishing.*
Knowling, Philip (2002)   Dartmoor Follies. *Orchard Publications.*
Newman, Philip (1992)   Tinners and Tenants on South-West Dartmoor.
Pearse, Colin (2004)   The Whitefaced Drift of Dartmoor's 'prapper' Sheep.
Piper, Hilda (1995)   Life at Narrator Farm. Dartmoor Newsletter. *Old Dartmoor Company.*

Rendell, Paul (1989) Sheepstor – A Study of Population Change in the 19th & 20th Centuries. *Old Dartmoor Company.*

Rendell, Paul (1989) Population at Eylesbarrow Tin Mine 1814-1852. *Plymouth Mineral and Mining Club Journal.*

Rendell, Paul (1993) The Grand Creber Tour. Published Privately

Rendell, Paul (1993) The Farms and Dwellings in the Parishes of Sheepstor and Walkhampton. *Published Privately.*

Rendell, Paul (1993 –1995) One by One they left the Valley. A series of articles in the Dartmoor Newsletter. *Old Dartmoor Company.*

Walsh, Peter & Byng Brian, Burrator: A pictorial History (1985) *Published Privately.*

Kelly's Directory - Various
White's Directory (1850)
Various issues of the Dartmoor News (1991-2007)
Various issues of the Western Morning News

RESOURCES

Ailsborough Mine's Cash Book
Memories of local people
Plymouth & West Devon Record Office
Local Studies Library, Plymouth
West Country Studies Library, Exeter
Census Returns 1851- 1891
South West Water Archives
Sites & Monuments Register, Exeter
Sheepstor Churchwardens Accounts
Tithe Map & Apportionments for Sheepstor and Walkhampton
Ledgers of the Manor of Walkhampton
Letter to Mr P. Barrett, Burrator Reservoir 30th Jan 1924 (PWDRO – 1646/258)
Newspaper cutting 1925 (PWDRO – 1646/382-387)

INDEX

Bal Mine 35
Ball Cottage 35
Burrator Halt 41, 42
Burrator Lodge 35
Burrator Reservoir 5,7,8,10,11, 41

Chipstone 10
Classeywell Cross 40
Classeywell Farm 14, 18, 51, 54
Classeywell Pool 14, 40, 50, 54
Combeshead Brook 13, 47
Combeshead Farm 12, 13, 54
Cuckoo Rock 15, 46

Deancombe Farm 15, 16, 31, 45, 54
Devonport Leat 41, 52
Drake Leat 7

Essworthy Farm 16, 54
Eylesbarrow Mine 18, 47

Headweir Cottage 36
Harris 26

Keaglesborough Mine 49, 52
Kingsett Farm 17, 18, 19, 20, 32, 49, 55

Leathertor Bridge 53
Leathertor Farm 20, 34, 52, 55
Longstone Manor 37, 38
Lowery 20, 21, 22, 23, 25, 55

Middleworth Farm 14, 24, 35, 45
Mullacroft Cottage 25, 26
Mullacroft Farm 25, 26, 56

Narrator Farm 19, 26, 27, 28, 48, 56
Newleycombe Farm 18, 28, 56
Nosworthy Bridge 19, 33
Nosworthy Farm 18, 29, 30, 56

Outholme Farm 30, 31, 56

Park Cottage Inn 13, 39
Potato Cave 46, 52
Plymouth Leat 7
Princetown Railway 41

Redstone Farm 10, 31, 57
Revolution 13, 46
Riddipit Farm 31, 57
Roundypark Farm 32, 57

Sheepstor 19
Stenlake Farm 32, 33, 52, 57

Vinneylake 33, 34, 57

THE AUTHOR

Paul Rendell was born in Plymouth and became enthusiastic about Dartmoor from an early age, especially its industrial archaeology and the wildlife, after being taken on numerous outings by his parents. Burrator and Sheepstor were two of the favourite places they went as a family.

Because he is dyslexic his schooldays were not very easy for him but he struggled on until school leaving age. After leaving school, Paul trained as a chef and worked in a number of establishments within the Plymouth area, as well as some on Dartmoor. Later on he became the Head Gardener at Devonport Dockyard and stayed there for several years but his love for Dartmoor led him to look for work away from the city. His boyhood explorations had already provided him with a knowledge of the moor that only a few possess and his interest led to a second job leading guided walks and giving talks. Through sheer grit and determination he became a full-time professional guide; this in turn has enabled him to introduce countless people to the delights of walking on Dartmoor and throughout the West Country.

As a keen local historian, Paul has written many articles for newspapers and magazines and wrote his first book 'Exploring the Lower Walkham Valley' in 1996. In 1991 he founded the 'Dartmoor News', a bi-monthly magazine which he still edits today. He is frequently out and about gathering information on matters relating to Dartmoor as well being the Bracken Officer for the Dartmoor Preservation Association, a Committee member for the Okehampton & District Branch of the Devonshire Association and is the editor of the 'Dartmoor Railway Newsletter'. He loves taking photographs and many of his pictures can be found on Christmas cards, postcards, calendars and in magazines. In his spare time he loves to collect old-picture postcards, listen to music and continues to explore the countryside.